I LOVE

The Great Smoky Mountains

Carole Ayres

Crippled Beagle Publishing
dyer.cbpublishing@gmail.com

©2018 Carole Ayres. All rights reserved.
Book design by Jody Dyer

Photo credits: **Carole Ayres** and Jody Dyer unless otherwise listed below.
Black bear cubs: https://www.flickr.com/photos/usfwssoutheast/26905180256
Map Image: https://commons.wikimedia.org/wiki/File:Map_of_Great_Smoky_Mountains_National_Park.png
Male deer: https://www.pexels.com/photo/deer-fall-great-smokey-mountains-smokey-mountains-600562/
Alum Cave Trail: Scott Basford (Blinutne) [GFDL (http://www.gnu.org/copyleft/fdl.html),
CC-BY-SA-3.0 (http://creativecommons.org/licenses/by-sa/3.0/)
Appalachian Trail: https://commons.wikimedia.org/wiki/File:Appalachian_Trail_at_Newfound_Gap.JPG
Boulders along Rainbow Falls: CC BY-SA 3.0, https://commons.wikimedia.org/w/index.php?curid=842996
Rainbow Falls CCL: https://en.wikipedia.org/wiki/Rainbow_Falls_Trail
Cabins on Mt. LeConte: https://www.flickr.com/photos/greatsmokymountainsnationalpark/40540420224
LeConte cabins in day: https://www.flickr.com/photos/jacobresor/32676799520
Stream: https://www.goodfreephotos.com
Alum Cave bluff: https://commons.wikimedia.org/wiki/File:Alum-cave-bluffs-tn1.jpg 19 June 2006, Brian Stansberry
Smoky Mountain Sunset: https://www.maxpixel.net/Great-Smoky-Mountains-Great-Smoky-Beautiful-3741390

ISBN-13: 978-1-970037-13-5

For my favorite cubs: Caroline, Campbell, Carson, Charlie, Sadie, Kade, and Keegan

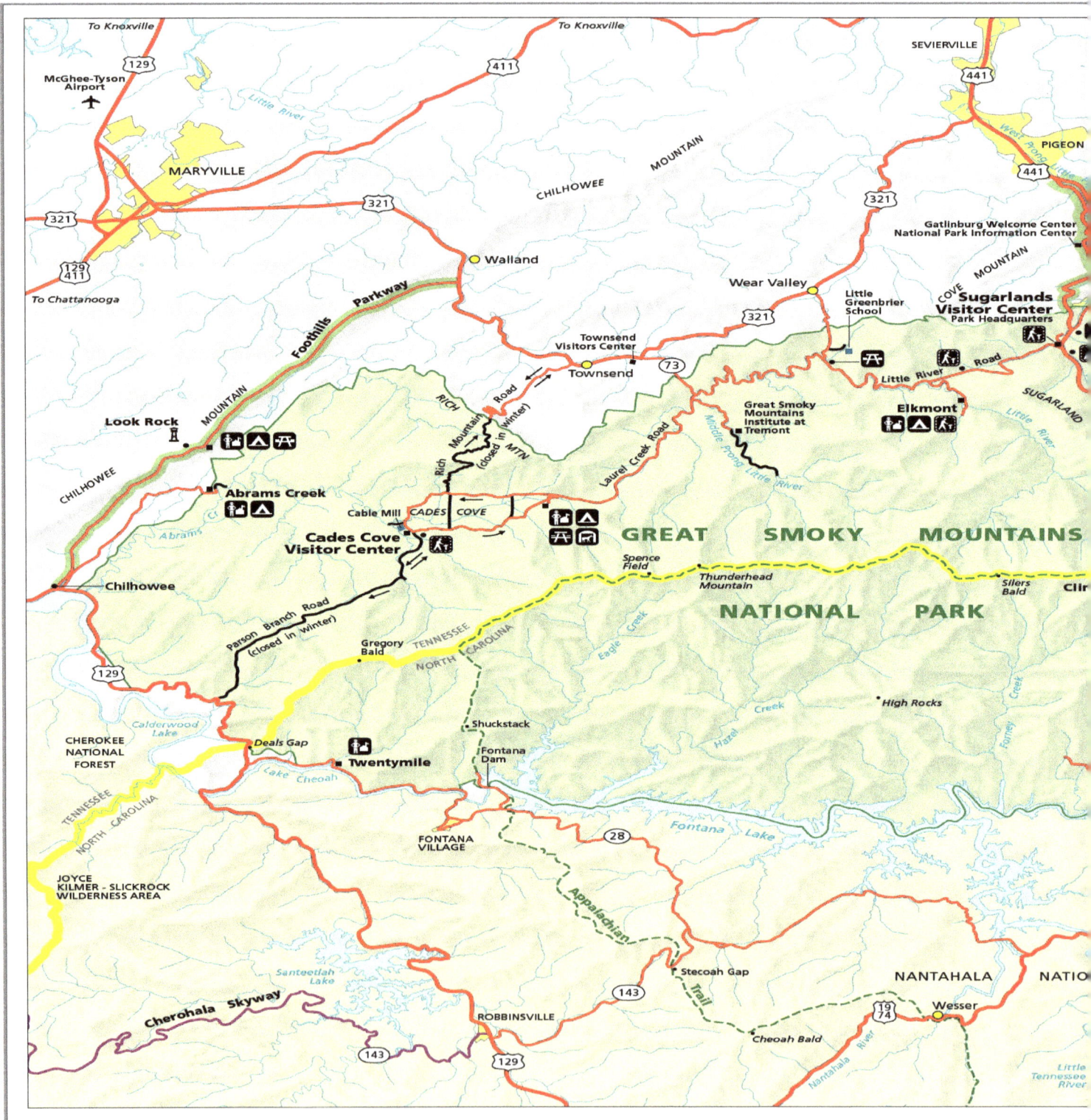

To Knoxville

129

McGhee-Tyson
Airport

411
To Knoxville

SEVIERVILLE

441

PIGEON

MARYVILLE

321

CHILHOWEE

MOUNTAIN

441

321

Gatlinburg Welcome Center
National Park Information Center

129
411
To Chattanooga

Foothills   Parkway

Walland

Wear Valley

321

Little
Greenbrier
School

COVE   MOUNTAIN

Sugarlands
Visitor Center
Park Headquarters

Townsend
Visitors Center

73

Townsend

Little River   Road

SUGARLAND

Look Rock

CHILHOWEE   MOUNTAIN

RICH   Mountain   Road
(closed in winter)

Great Smoky
Mountains
Institute at
Tremont

Laurel Creek Road

Middle Prong Little River

Elkmont

Little River

Abrams Creek

Abrams

Cable Mill

CADES   COVE

Cades Cove
Visitor Center

GREAT   SMOKY   MOUNTAINS

Spence
Field

Chilhowee

Parson Branch Road
(closed in winter)

Gregory
Bald

TENNESSEE
NORTH CAROLINA

Thunderhead
Mountain

NATIONAL   PARK

Silers
Bald   Clin

Eagle   Creek

129

Calderwood
Lake

Shuckstack

High Rocks

Hazel   Creek

Forney   Creek

CHEROKEE
NATIONAL
FOREST

Deals Gap

Lake Cheoah

Twentymile

Fontana
Dam

TENNESSEE
NORTH CAROLINA

28

Fontana   Lake

FONTANA
VILLAGE

JOYCE
KILMER – SLICKROCK
WILDERNESS AREA

Santeetlah
Lake

Appalachian

NANTAHALA   NATIO

Cherohala   Skyway

143

Stecoah Gap

Trail

19
74

Wesser

ROBBINSVILLE

143

129

Cheoah Bald

Nantahala   River

Little
Tennessee
River

To Newport

321

32

Foothills Parkway
(closed in winter)

Cosby

Exit 443

Pigeon

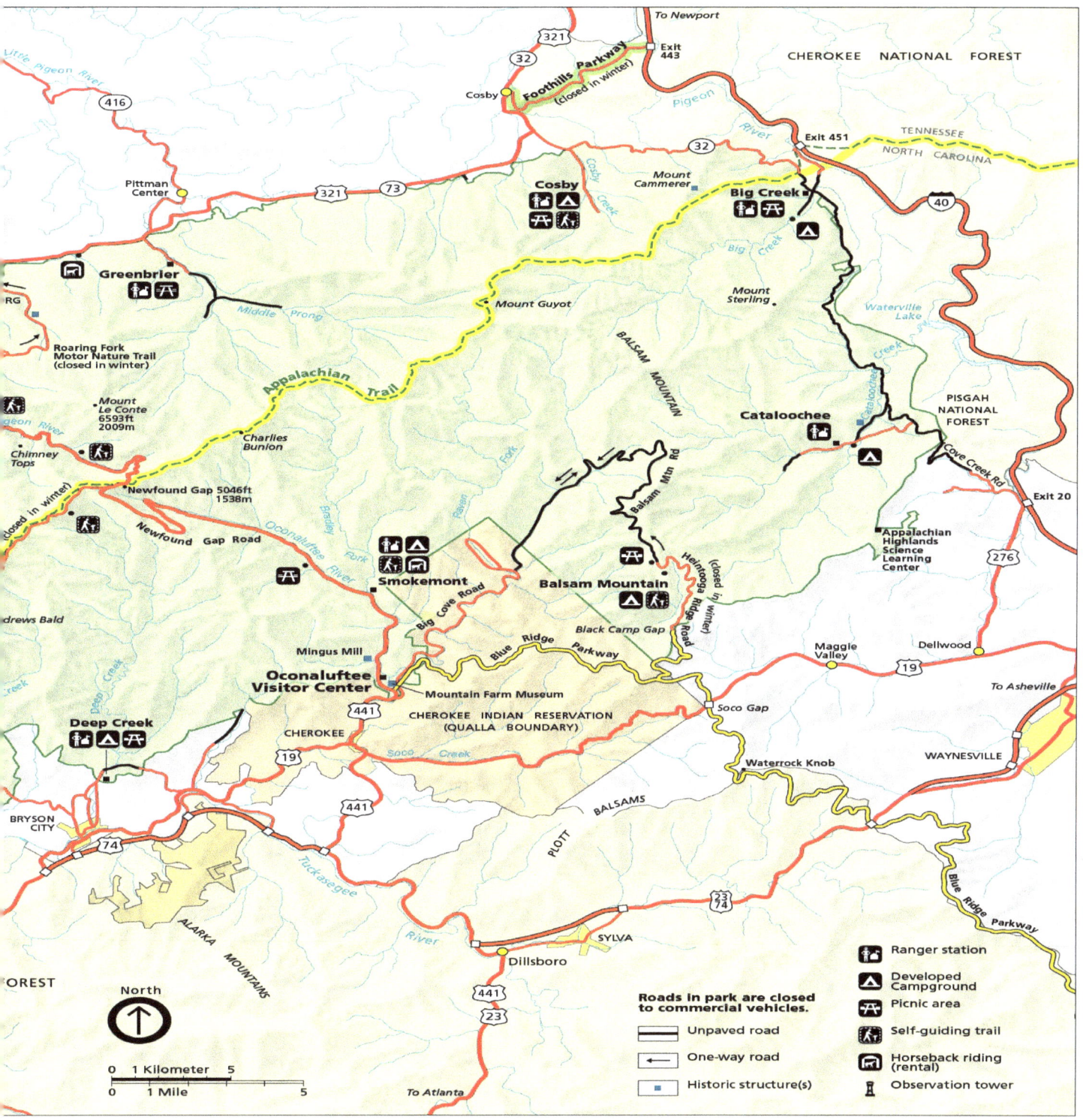

CHEROKEE NATIONAL FOREST

416

321   73

32

Exit 451

TENNESSEE

NORTH CAROLINA

40

Pittman
Center

Cosby

Mount
Cammerer

Cosby Creek

Mount
Sterling

Big Creek

Big Creek

Waterville
Lake

Greenbrier

RG

Middle   Prong

Appalachian   Trail

Mount Guyot

BALSAM   MOUNTAIN

Cataloochee

Cataloochee Creek

PISGAH
NATIONAL
FOREST

Roaring Fork
Motor Nature Trail
(closed in winter)

Mount
Le Conte
6593ft
2009m

Charlies
Bunion

Cove Creek Rd

Exit 20

Chimney
Tops

Pigeon River

Newfound Gap 5046ft
1538m

Bradley Fork

Oconaluftee River

Balsam Mtn Rd

Appalachian
Highlands
Science
Learning
Center

276

(closed in winter)

Newfound   Gap   Road

Smokemont

Balsam Mountain

Heintooga Ridge Road

drews Bald

Deep Creek

Black Camp Gap

Maggie
Valley

Dellwood

To Asheville

Mingus Mill

Big Cove Road

Blue Ridge   Parkway

19

Oconaluftee
Visitor Center

Mountain Farm Museum

441

CHEROKEE

CHEROKEE   INDIAN   RESERVATION
(QUALLA   BOUNDARY)

Soco Gap

Deep Creek

Soco   Creek

Waterrock Knob

WAYNESVILLE

BRYSON
CITY

19

441

BALSAMS

74

Tuckasegee

PLOTT

23
74

Blue Ridge Parkway

ALARKA   MOUNTAINS

River

SYLVA

OREST

North

Dillsboro

Roads in park are closed
to commercial vehicles.

Ranger station

441

23

Unpaved road

Developed
Campground

0   1 Kilometer   5

One-way road

Picnic area

0   1 Mile   5

Historic structure(s)

Self-guiding trail

To Atlanta

Horseback riding
(rental)

Observation tower

Let's drive to the Smoky Mountains and head for the trail.

When we get out of the car, take a deep breath and exhale.

Look up at the trees and down the narrow path at our feet.

The quiet breeze is all we hear. We're in for an amazing treat.

We are not sure where this path will lead us; it's true,
But a waterfall would give us an exquisite view.
Water tumbling and splashing, flowing over the rocks,
Climbing slick stones will give us wet shoes and socks.

The water is silver, and the rocks are large and gray.
Cushiony green moss at the edge
gives us a soft place to play.
Look up at the sun sparkling through the moving leaves.
We found a great spot to lie down whenever we please.

We lie on our back's, take a deep breath; it's true.
God's peaceful forest is an extravagant gift just for you.

APPALACHIAN TRAIL

Sweat Heifer Creek Trail	1.7
Icewater Spring Shelter	2.9
Charlies Bunion	4.0
Mount LeConte	8.0

When we wake up,
Well rested we will be.
The path climbs upward.
There's much more to see.

We will wind around big boulders
And step over tree roots.
Seems like the route winds uphill
Wherever it suits.
Long, long ago the deer who made this trail
Were hunted by Indians
Before the deer scent got stale.

At Alum Cave we sit down in the dust for a long rest.
We eat trail mix, drink water, and swat a few pests.
We ponder, *Did the Indians sleep here to get out of the rain?*
Did a creek form here to help the rain drain?

The sun is sinking lower in the cloudless sky.
The air is getting cooler as we climb ever high.
So on the trail ever higher we still go.
When we get there, God will deliver a spectacular show.

We are worn out,
But need to climb to the top.
To arrive in time for the sunset,
We'd better not stop.

As we round the last bend,
The sun begins to set.
Our cabin mates greet us,
We breathe in the sunset.

Peacefully, we watch the last rays of the sun with friends.

On the top of Mount LeConte, God's peace descends.

In the dining hall at Mount LeConte,
We take our seats,
Enjoy the yummy stew,
And fellowship until we retreat.

In our cabin, we laugh a lot.
We tell stories and share,
Resting in the knowledge,
We are kept in God's constant care.

As we climb in our bunk beds
And settle to rest on our backs,
We fall asleep listening to mice pull
Treats from our packs.

Dear reader,
I hope someday soon you will go
To the Smoky Mountains to see
one of nature's glorious shows.

About the Author

Carole Ayres lives in Tennessee, USA, with her husband and world-traveling companion Joe. She's a retired teacher who loves to spend time outdoors with her seven grandchildren and share her passion for travel and discovery with young people.

Look for other *I LOVE* books by Carole Ayres on Amazon.com, Kindle, Barnes & Noble, and at retail bookstores. For information on future titles, book signings, and interviews, contact the publisher: dyer.cbpublishing@gmail.com

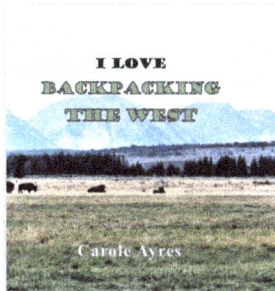

I LOVE BACKPACKING THE WEST — Carole Ayres

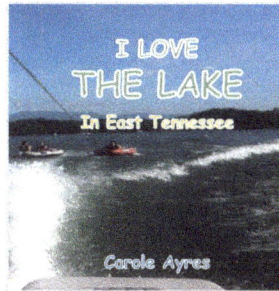

I LOVE THE LAKE In East Tennessee — Carole Ayres

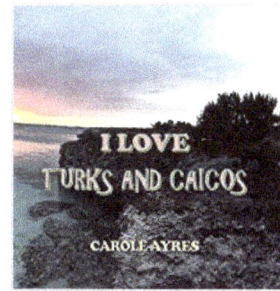

I LOVE TURKS AND CAICOS — CAROLE AYRES

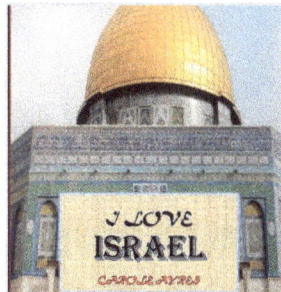

I LOVE ISRAEL — CAROLE AYRES

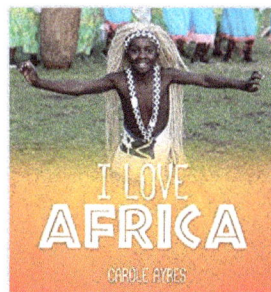

I LOVE AFRICA — CAROLE AYRES

www.ingramcontent.com/pod-product-compliance
Lightning Source LLC
Chambersburg PA
CBHW051324020426
42333CB00032B/3476